Cal Can Bat

by Tristan Horrom
illustrated by Kate Flanagan

Decodable 5

McGraw Hill Education

Bothell, WA • Chicago, IL • Columbus, OH • New York, NY

MHEonline.com

Send all inquiries to:
McGraw-Hill Education
8787 Orion Place
Columbus, OH 43240

ISBN: 978-0-02-144983-5
MHID: 0-02-144983-X

Printed in China

9 10 11 12 13 DSS 28 27 26 25 24

Cal is at bat.

Tim tips his cap.

It is past Cal.

His pal claps.

Can Cal hit it?

Cal can!

Cal hit it!